patchwork loves
embroidery

patchwork loves embroidery

hand stitches, pretty projects

GAIL PAN

Martingale®
Create with Confidence

Patchwork Loves Embroidery: Hand Stitches, Pretty Projects
© 2014 by Gail Pan

Martingale®
19021 120th Ave. NE, Ste. 102
Bothell, WA 98011-9511 USA
ShopMartingale.com

Printed in China

19 18 17 16 15 14   8 7 6 5 4 3 2 1

Library of Congress Cataloging-in-Publication Data is available upon request.

ISBN: 978-1-60468-373-8

Mission Statement

Dedicated to providing quality products and service to inspire creativity.

Credits

PRESIDENT AND CEO: Tom Wierzbicki
EDITOR IN CHIEF: Mary V. Green
DESIGN DIRECTOR: Paula Schlosser
MANAGING EDITOR: Karen Costello Soltys
ACQUISITIONS EDITOR: Karen M. Burns
TECHNICAL EDITOR: Laura Stone Roberts
COPY EDITOR: Marcy Heffernan
PRODUCTION MANAGER: Regina Girard
COVER AND INTERIOR DESIGNER: Paula Schlosser
PHOTOGRAPHER: Brent Kane
ILLUSTRATOR: Rose Wright

contents

introduction

My name is Gail Pan, and I am an embroiderer and quilter from Australia. I have a great affection for (and addiction to) fabric and thread and love to spend time stitching with friends or at home on the couch, bringing fabric and thread together. Most of my designs are inspired by my surroundings, from my home and garden to the things I see when out and about on my daily walk. And, of course, beautiful fabric is always a great inspiration, too!

I hope to bring you some enjoyment with the projects in this book. They were designed to blend a passion for both embroidery and patchwork. From the smallest pincushion or bag to the larger projects like the "Bless My Garden Wall Quilt," you'll see that none of them is so large that the patchwork ovewhelms the embroidered designs. All of the projects are meant to be used and savored in your daily life so you can delight in the designs up close. And you'll find that there is something just right for both the beginning and the experienced embroiderer.

Please don't be afraid to mix and match the projects. If you want to sew a bag, but love the embroidery design on one of the quilts, go ahead and use the design on the bag. After all, it's going to be yours! Make the projects personal. Feel free to choose your own color schemes. Please yourself.

I hope you enjoy the ideas in this book and find the stitching most relaxing and gratifying. If you find joy in fabric and thread already, then maybe you will become addicted to both embroidery and patchwork, just like me!

general instructions

The projects in this book combine hand embroidery with piecing and hand quilting. In this section, I'll review some of the basic information you'll need, but if you're new to sewing and quilting, you can find additional helpful information for free at ShopMartingale.com/HowtoQuilt, where you can download illustrated how-to guides on everything from rotary cutting to binding a quilt.

Embroidery Instructions

There are many different styles and techniques in the embroidery world. Give yourself the gift of trying as many ways to embroider as you can. This way you'll find the stitches, threads, fabrics, and techniques that work well for you and that you enjoy the most. In this book, I'm sharing some of the techniques I like best, along with designs that make me happy and that I hope will bring a smile to your face.

NEEDLES

You can find so many types of hand-sewing needles on the market, each designed for a different technique. Needle packages are labeled by type and size. The larger the needle size, the smaller the needle (a size 1 needle will be longer and thicker than a size 12 needle). For embroidery, I like to use a size 8 embroidery needle (also referred to as a crewel needle). An embroidery needle is similar to a Sharp, but with an elongated eye designed to accommodate six-strand floss or pearl cotton. You may prefer a size 7 or 9. For appliqué, I use a size 10 straw needle (also called a milliner's or appliqué needle), but a size 9 or 11 may be your preference. When hand quilting with size 8 pearl cotton, I prefer to use a size 5 or 6 embroidery needle. This allows me to thread the needle easily. You may find a smaller needle more helpful. Test a few needles until you find one that suits you; any brand is fine.

THREADS

I like to use a variety of threads. Some threads I select to match the fabrics I plan to use; sometimes I pick a thread first, and then choose appropriate fabrics. Six-strand embroidery floss is the most common floss used. It needs to be split before stitching since only two or three strands are used at once. I prefer to use two strands and have used two strands for most of the projects in this book. Some threads, such as the pearl cotton I use when quilting, can be used straight off the spool or ball. I always knot my threads when embroidering. Because the embroidered squares are backed with fusible interfacing before being stitched, I don't need to worry that the knots are going to show through. To start embroidering, I just thread my needle with the appropriate floss and make a knot at the end of the strand. When I have about 4" to 5" of floss left, or when I've completed stitching with a color, I keep the needle at the back of the embroidery. Then, I loop the thread around the needle and push the resulting knot close to the back of the stitch I have just finished.

My favorite threads for embroidery are Aurifil Mako Cotton 12-weight thread; 6-strand embroidery floss from Cosmo, DMC, and Weeks Dye Works; Gentle Arts sampler threads; and size 12 pearl cotton from DMC or Valdani. My favorite thread for quilting is DMC size 8 pearl cotton. I've used all of these threads in the projects in this book.

TRACING THE DESIGN

When it comes to tracing or transferring the embroidery design onto your fabric, I recommend using a light box. Tape the design in place on the light box, and then center the fabric on top of the design and secure it in place. Use a brown fine-point Pigma pen to trace lightly over the design. A fine-point washable marker, a ceramic pencil (such as Sewline), or a mechanical or wooden pencil with a fine, hard lead will also work.

If you don't have a light box, you can tape the design to a window or use a glass-topped table with a lamp underneath. I always trace the minimum. For instance, if you're tracing lazy daisy stitches (loops on the embroidery pattern), only mark a dot where you will start the stitch. Leave dotted lines (running stitches) untraced, stitching where they appear by referring to the illustration or photo. Trace only the straight line for blanket stitching. You'll soon find the sort of marking that will work best for you.

EMBROIDERY FABRIC AND INTERFACING

For easier tracing, choose a light-colored fabric for the background. It's OK to use a subtle print, such as a small polka dot; the print will add some interest. Tone-on-tone fabrics are also nice to use. Some patterns call for handkerchief linen. This is a very lightweight, finely woven linen.

I always back my traced fabric with a very lightweight fusible interfacing. This serves to prevent show-through of the embroidery threads and knots. And, because the interfacing stiffens the fabric a bit, there is less distortion of the fabric and stitches when the embroidered piece is hooped. To do as I do, cut a piece of interfacing the same size and shape as your background fabric and, following the manufacturer's instructions, fuse it in place *after* you've traced the design and *before* you start stitching.

HOOPS

I use an embroidery hoop to keep the fabric taut, but not tight, while stitching. Hoops are available in wood, metal, and plastic, with different mechanisms for keeping the fabric taut. Any type of hoop is fine, so take the time to find one you're comfortable with. A 4" hoop is my preferred size, but you may prefer a 5" or 6" hoop. Remember to always remove your fabric from the hoop when you've finished stitching for the day.

Embroidery Stitches

Backstitch

Blanket stitch

Cross-stitch

French knot

Lazy daisy stitch

Running stitch

Satin stitch

Stem stitch

Sewing and Quilting Instructions

Please read through the instructions carefully before starting. For all projects, the yardage is based on 42"-wide fabric, the seam allowances are always ¼", and I usually press the seam allowances *away* from the embroidered fabric and toward the darker fabrics.

BATTING

I like to use cotton batting in all my quilts. For smaller projects, such as the "Cinnamon Delights Bag" (page 20) or the "Garden Delight Needle Book" (page 39), a lightweight batting is preferable. Fiberfill and/or crushed walnut shells are used in the pincushions. See "Why Walnut Shells?" on page 18 for more information.

APPLIQUÉ

For some projects in this book I've embroidered the design onto the background fabric first, and then used needle-turn appliqué to stitch it in place on the appropriate item. If you wish to do likewise, trace the appliqué line onto the background fabric when tracing the design. Once you've finished the stitching, cut out the embroidered design, leaving a scant ¼" seam allowance from the appliqué line.

On inner curves, clip into the seam allowance up to, but not through, the marked line. Avoiding the edges, baste the embroidery in position with appliqué glue. Roxanne's Glue-Baste-It is my favorite appliqué glue because it enables me to place tiny, controlled dots of glue exactly where I want them, and it's also 100% water soluble. Working an inch or two at a time, use the tip of the needle to turn under the seam allowance along the marked line, and secure it in place using thread that matches the appliqué fabric and very small slip stitches or blind stitches.

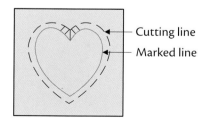
— Cutting line
— Marked line

QUILTING

To add a little dimension to my projects, I use big-stitch and size 8 ecru pearl cotton to hand quilt my projects. I begin by placing ¼" quilter's tape so that one side adjoins a seam line or other feature of my project, such as an embroidered circle. Stitching along the other edge of the tape allows me to stitch a quilting line that is even and exactly ¼" from the seam. Quilter's tape comes on a roll and is both inexpensive and repositionable.

Thread your needle with the end straight off the ball, and cut the thread to about 15" long. Knot one end with a single knot. Insert your needle through the backing fabric to the front, where you want to start. Pull the backing fabric away from the batting and pull on the thread. Tug gently so the knot pops into the layers. Bring the needle up through the quilt top right next to your ¼" quilter's tape, and then insert it back into the quilt right next to the ¼" tape and approximately ¼" from the spot where your needle came up. This will make a big stitch approximately ¼" long. Bring the needle back up next to the tape and ¼" from the point where the needle went down last. Continue in this manner until your thread is approximately 4" to 5" long. Take the thread to the back, knot the thread, and then pull the knot back into the quilt, between the backing and the batting, bringing the needle out approximately 1" away. Trim the thread close to the backing fabric.

BINDING

For big quilts and larger projects, such as "Willow Tree Lane Wall Quilt" (page 12), I use 2½"-wide fabric strips to make double-fold binding. Cut the number of strips listed for binding in the pattern, and then sew the strips together end to end. Press the seam allowances open. Fold over one end of the strip at a 45° angle to form the start, and then fold the strip in half lengthwise, wrong sides together. Place the starting end of the binding on the front of the quilt, at least 8" from a corner, and with the raw edges of the quilt and the folded strip aligned. Begin to sew the binding to the quilt a few inches from the folded end of the binding. Continue to stitch the binding to the quilt, mitering the corners as you go. When you're a few inches from the start, trim the end of your strip to the length needed to tuck it into the folded end of the strip beginning. Fold the beginning end of the strip over the tucked-in end, and aligning raw edges, sew the last few inches of the binding to the quilt. Fold the binding over to the back and slip-stitch it in place.

Joining straight-cut strips

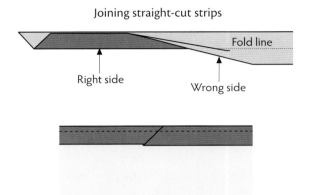

For smaller projects, such as the needle book, a wide, double-fold binding is too bulky, so I use a single-fold binding instead. For single-fold binding, cut fabric strips 1½" wide. Stitch the strips together and press the seam allowances open as for 2½"-wide binding. Press under ¼" along one long edge to form a fold. (This edge will be turned to the back of the quilt and sewn in place once the binding is attached to the front.) Fold under ¼" twice at one end of the strip to

form a finished edge. Sew the raw edge of the binding to the quilt as for double-fold binding. When you get back to the beginning, trim the binding strip so that it overlaps the folded start by ¼" to ½". Continue sewing over the lapped binding until you've reached the stitching at the beginning. Fold the binding to the back of the quilt and slip-stitch the pressed edge of the binding in place. For long strips on the needle book and other folders, tuck in the ends before folding in place. Hold with binder clips or pins while you slip-stitch the binding in place.

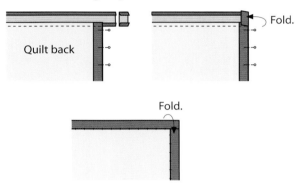

willow tree lane wall quilt

Take a trip down Willow Tree Lane with its
whimsical houses and gorgeous willow trees.

Materials

Yardage is based on 42"-wide fabric unless otherwise noted.

⅝ yard of light-green print for blocks and binding

½ yard of cream solid for embroidered blocks

½ yard of red floral for blocks and outer border

½ yard of red tone on tone for blocks

⅜ yard of brown print for blocks

¼ yard of brown dot for inner border

1¼ yards of fabric for backing

41" x 41" piece of batting

1⅛ yards of lightweight fusible interfacing, 18" to 20" wide, for embroidery backing

6-strand embroidery floss in brown, red, yellow, and variegated sage green

Ecru pearl cotton, size 8

¼" quilter's tape (optional, see page 10)

Cutting

From the cream solid, cut:
2 strips, 7" x 42"; crosscut into 9 squares, 7" x 7"

From the lightweight fusible interfacing, cut:
9 squares, 7" x 7"

From the brown print, cut:
4 strips, 2½" x 42"; crosscut into 52 squares, 2½" x 2½"

From the red tone on tone, cut:
4 strips, 2½" x 42"; crosscut into:
 16 strips, 2½" x 6½"
 16 squares, 2½" x 2½"

From the red floral, cut:
2 strips, 2½" x 42"; crosscut into:
 8 strips, 2½" x 6½"
 8 squares, 2½" x 2½"
2 strips, 2½" x 32½"
2 strips, 2½" x 36½"

From the light-green print, cut:
2 strips, 2½" x 42"; crosscut into:
 8 strips, 2½" x 6½"
 8 squares, 2½" x 2½"
4 strips, 2½" x 42"

From the brown dot, cut:
2 strips, 1½" x 30½"
2 strips, 1½" x 32½"

Embroidering the Designs

1. Using the patterns on pages 15 and 16, trace the House design onto the right side of four of the cream squares and the Tree design onto the right side of the remaining five cream squares. Fuse an interfacing square to the wrong side of each marked square.

2. Using two strands of floss, embroider the designs, following the stitch key and color guides on the patterns.

Making the Blocks

1. Centering the embroidered design, trim the stitched squares to 6½" x 6½".

2. Mark a diagonal line on the *wrong* side of 36 brown 2½" squares. Aligning the corners, pin a marked square to an embroidered square, right sides together. Sew directly on the marked line. Trim ¼" outside the seam line and press the seam allowances as indicated. Repeat on all four corners

of each embroidered square to make a total of nine embroidered Snowball blocks.

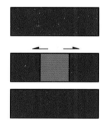 

Make 9.

3. For each pieced block you'll need a set of two matching 2½" squares and two matching 2½" x 6½" strips, plus one brown 2½" square. Sew the matching squares to opposite sides of the brown square and press the seam allowances away from the brown square. Sew the matching strips to either side of the pieced strip, and press the seam allowances away from the pieced strip to complete the block. Repeat to make eight red tone-on-tone blocks, four red-floral blocks, and four light-green blocks.

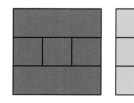

Make 8.

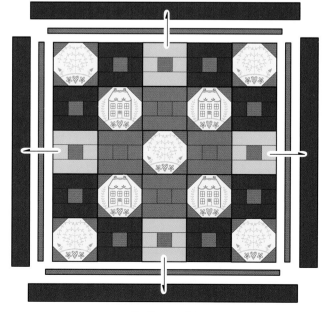

Make 4 of each.

Assembling the Quilt Top

Lay out five rows of five blocks each, making sure all embroidered blocks are upright. Sew the blocks together into rows, pressing the seam allowances in opposite directions from row to row. Sew the rows together and press.

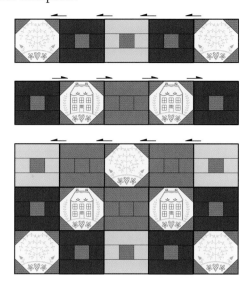

Adding the Borders

1. Sew a brown-dot 30½"-long strip to each side of the quilt top. Press the seam allowances toward the strips. Sew brown-dot 32½"-long strips to the top and bottom of the quilt top. Press the seam allowances toward the strips.

2. Sew a red-floral 32½"-long strip to each side of the quilt top. Press the seam allowances toward the red strips. Sew red-floral 36½"-long strips to the top and bottom of the quilt top. Press the seam allowances toward the floral strips.

Quilt assembly

Finishing the Quilt

1. Layer the quilt top, batting, and backing; baste. Using pearl cotton and big-stitch quilting (see page 10), quilt ¼" from the brown center square and ¼" from the seam line in each pieced block and in the borders.

2. Trim the batting and backing even with the top.

3. To make an optional hanging sleeve prior to binding, fold the ends of a 5" x 30" strip under ¼" twice and topstitch to hem. Fold the strip in half lengthwise, *wrong* sides together, and press. Aligning the raw edges, stitch the folded strip to the top of the quilt back, ⅛" from the raw edges.

4. Using the light-green 2½"-wide strips, make and attach the binding *before* completing the quilting next to the binding seam (do not quilt through the sleeve if there is one). Stitch the lower (folded) edge of the sleeve to the backing by hand.

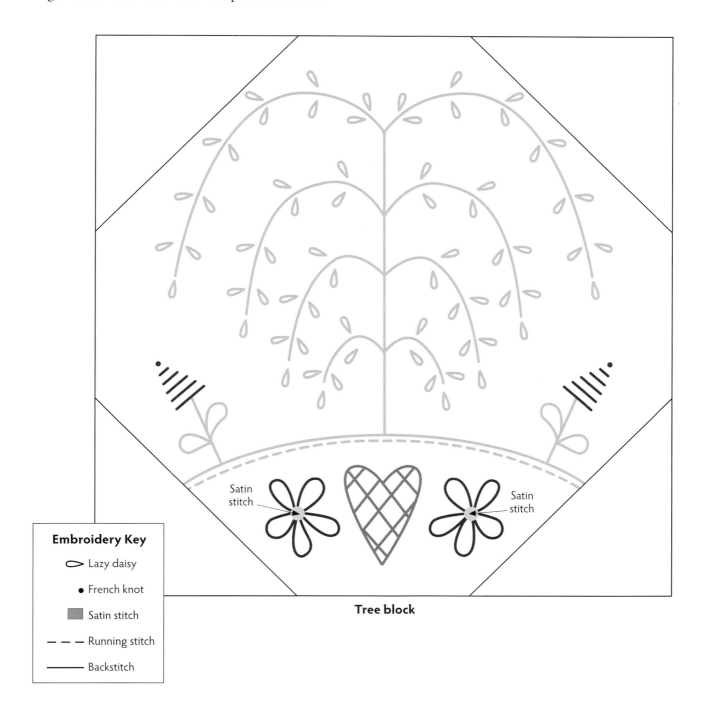

Satin stitch

Satin stitch

Tree block

Embroidery Key

⊂ Lazy daisy

• French knot

▨ Satin stitch

– – – Running stitch

——— Backstitch

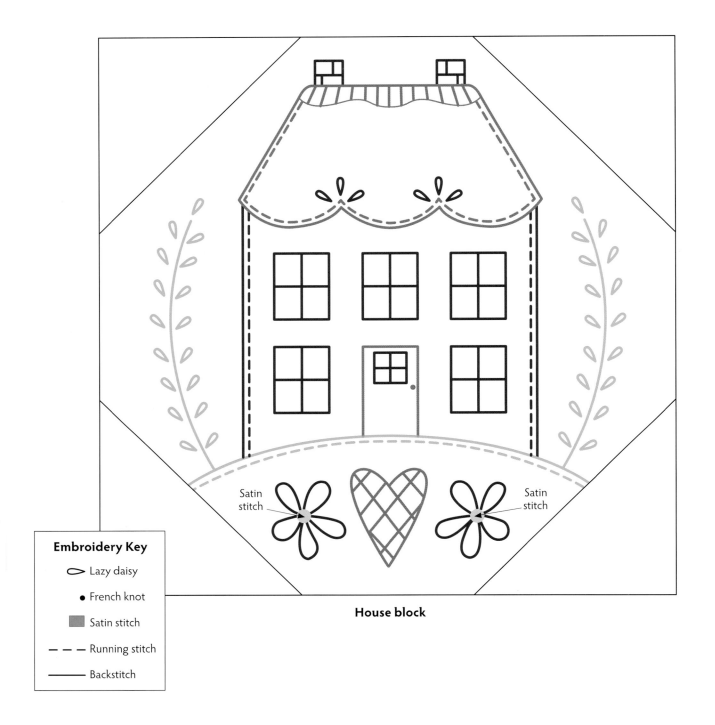

Embroidery Key

◯ Lazy daisy

● French knot

▨ Satin stitch

– – – Running stitch

—— Backstitch

Satin stitch

Satin stitch

House block

pretty bluebird pincushion

Bring a touch of happiness to your sewing room with this large pincushion, stitched with sweet flowers and a trio of whimsical bluebirds.

Materials

1 square, 10" x 10", of cream print for pincushion top

2 rectangles, 5" x 10", of red print for backing

1 square, 10" x 10", of lightweight fusible interfacing for embroidery backing

6-strand embroidery floss in red, pink, yellow, light green, dark green, light blue, and medium blue

1 cream button, 1" in diameter

Fiberfill and/or ground walnut shells for stuffing

Embroidering the Design

1. Using the pattern on page 19, trace the hexagon outline onto the *wrong* side of the cream-print square. Turn the square over and line up the drawn hexagon on the back of the square with the hexagon outline on the pattern. Trace the rest of the Pretty Bluebird design onto the *right* side of the fabric. Fuse the interfacing square to the wrong side of the marked square.

2. Using two strands of floss, embroider the design, following the stitch key and color guides on the pattern.

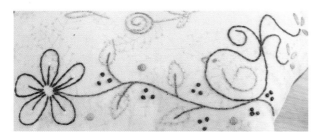

Assembling the Pincushion

1. Using a ¼" seam allowance and with wrong sides facing, sew the two red rectangles together along one long edge, leaving a 2"-wide opening in the center of the seam for turning. Press the seam allowances to one side.

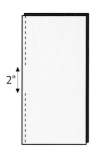 

2. Lay the embroidered square on the pieced backing, right sides together. Pin the layers together, and then sew on the hexagon outline all the way around, overlapping stitching at the beginning and end of the seam to secure. Trim ¼" from the stitched line. Trim the corners.

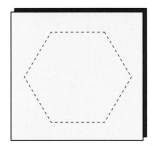

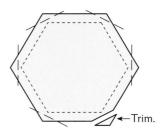

←Trim.

Trim ¼" from stitch line.

3. Turn the pincushion right side out through the opening. Stuff firmly with fiberfill and/or walnut shells. Hand stitch the opening closed.

4. Sew a button to the center of the pincushion by inserting a threaded needle into the center of the pincushion bottom and bringing it up through the center of the top, leaving a 3" to 4" tail of thread on the bottom. Stitch through the button, and then back through the pincushion to the bottom two or three times, pulling the thread taut so the button is secure and the surface of the pincushion is indented slightly. Knot the threads together on the bottom and bury the tails in the pincushion.

Why Walnut Shells?

Crushed walnut shells add weight to the pincushion and help to keep your pins sharp and clean. I like to make a layer, approximately ½" thick, of walnut shells at the top of the pincushion and then pack it tightly with fiberfill.

Satin stitch

Satin stitch

Embroidery Key

⟜ Lazy daisy

• French knot

▨ Satin stitch

— Backstitch

Pretty Bluebird Pincushion

cinnamon delights bag

This cute and handy little bag is embroidered
with a delicious shade of cinnamon floss.

Materials

Yardage is based on 42"-wide fabric. Fat eighths measure 9" x 21".

¼ yard of beige print for lining

1 fat eighth of blue print for bag front and back

1 fat eighth of rust print for bag front and back

1 square, 5" x 5", of cream print for embroidery background

2 rectangles, 9½" x 11", of thin batting

1 square, 5" x 5", of lightweight fusible interfacing for embroidery backing

1½ yards of ¼"-diameter cream cord

6-strand embroidery floss in cinnamon

Ecru pearl cotton, size 8

Template plastic

¼" quilter's tape (optional, see page 10)

Appliqué basting glue

Cutting

From the blue print, cut:

2 rectangles, 7½" x 8½"

From the rust print, cut:

2 rectangles, 3½" x 8½"

2 strips, 1¼" x 7"

From the beige print, cut:

2 rectangles, 8½" x 10½"

Embroidering the Circle

1. Using the pattern on page 23, trace the Cinnamon Delights design onto the right side of the cream-print square. Trace the circle also; this is your appliqué line. Fuse the interfacing to the back of the marked square.

2. Using two strands of floss, embroider the design, following the stitch key on the pattern.

Making the Bag Front and Back

1. Sew a blue 7½" x 8½" rectangle and a rust 3½" x 8½" rectangle together along their 8½" edges to make a pieced rectangle. Press the seam allowances toward the rust fabric. Repeat to make a second pieced rectangle.

2. Cut out the embroidered circle ¼" beyond the marked appliqué line to create a ¼" turn-under allowance.

3. With the design upright, position the circle so the appliqué line is 3" from the top (blue) edge of a pieced rectangle and the circle is centered between the sides. Glue baste it in place by applying two pinhead-sized dots of appliqué glue about an inch apart near the middle of the circle. Using needle-turn appliqué, stitch the circle in place, turning the edge under just until the appliqué line is no longer visible.

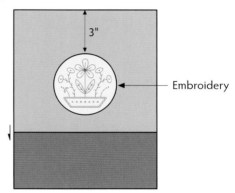

Quilting the Bag Front and Back

1. Baste the front of the bag to one of the batting pieces. Trace the quilting design on page 23 onto template plastic and cut it out on the line.

2. Place the template over the appliquéd circle and, using a white ceramic pencil, draw around the shape to mark the quilting line. Quilt on the line using big-stitch quilting (see page 10) and pearl cotton. Quilt ¼" from each side of the seam line. Trim the batting even with the fabrics.

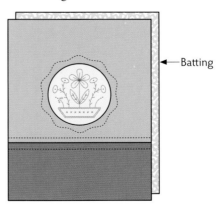

3. Baste the remaining pieced rectangle (bag back) to the remaining piece of batting and quilt ¼" from each side of the seam line as before. Trim the batting even with the fabric.

Assembling the Bag

1. To make a casing, fold under ¼" on both long sides of a rust 1¼" x 7" strip and press. With the long edges pressed under, fold under ¼" on both ends of the strip and press. Repeat to make the second casing.

2. Position one casing on the bag front, 1¼" down from the top raw edge and an equal distance from each side. Pin in place. Backstitching at each end to secure, topstitch each long edge of the casing in

place, leaving the ends open. Pull the threads to the back and tie off. Trim the threads. Repeat for the bag back.

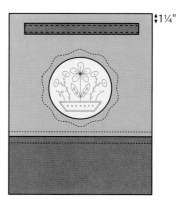

1¼"

3. Pin the bag back and front right sides together. Using a ¼" seam allowance, sew down one side of the bag, across the bottom, and up the other side. With the bag still wrong side out, box one bottom corner by bringing the bottom seam together with a side seam. Press flat and pin. Measure 2" from the corner and draw a line perpendicular to the

Easy Casings

Use a little appliqué glue to hold the folded ends of the casings in place after pressing.

seams. Sew along this line and then trim ¼" from the stitching line. Repeat for the other corner.

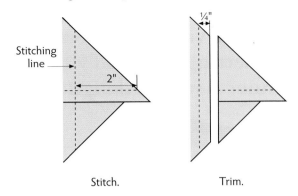

Stitch. Trim.

4. Pin the lining rectangles right sides together. Using a ¼" seam allowance, sew down one long side and across the bottom, leaving a 3" opening for turning, and up the other long side. Leave the top open. Box the corners of the lining as you did for the bag. Do not turn the lining right side out.

5. Place the outer bag inside the lining, right sides together and matching the side seams. Pin along the top raw edge. Sew around the top edge. Turn

the bag right side out through the opening in the lining. Slip-stitch the opening closed. Push the lining into the bag, smooth it out, and then press. Edgestitch ⅛" from the top edge.

Finishing the Bag

Cut the cord in half to make two equal lengths. Thread one of the lengths through one casing and around and through the other. Tie the cord ends in a knot. Repeat for the remaining length, starting at the opposite side of the bag. Pull the cords to close the bag.

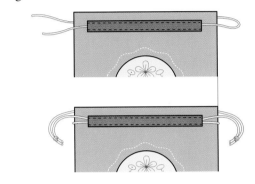

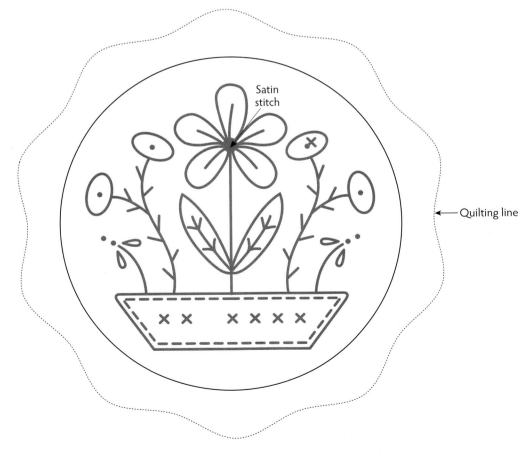

Embroidery Key

◡ Lazy daisy

● French knot

✕✕ Cross-stitch

▨ Satin stitch

– – – Running stitch

——— Backstitch

Cinnamon Delights Bag

lovebirds table runner

Little blue lovebirds nestled among a vine of glorious flowers make for a romantic table setting. Stitched with lovely soft colors, this table runner is sure to delight.

Materials

Yardage is based on 42"-wide fabric unless otherwise noted.

½ yard of red dot for sashing strips and binding

⅜ yard of blue floral for strips and outer border

⅜ yard of cream dot for embroidery background

¼ yard of brown tone on tone for inner border

¾ yard of fabric for backing

22" x 38" piece of batting

½ yard of lightweight fusible interfacing, 18" to 20" wide, for embroidery backing

6-strand embroidery floss in green, red, pink, yellow, teal, and light gray

Ecru pearl cotton, size 8

¼" quilter's tape (optional, see page 10)

Cutting

From the cream dot, cut:

1 rectangle, 10" x 12"

2 strips, 4" x 12"

From the lightweight fusible interfacing, cut:

1 rectangle, 10" x 12"

2 strips, 4" x 12"

From the red dot, cut:

3 strips, 1½" x 42"; crosscut into:

    2 strips, 1½" x 13½"

    4 strips, 1½" x 11½"

    2 strips, 1½" x 9½"

3 strips, 2½" x 42"

From the blue floral, cut:

2 strips, 2½" x 42"; crosscut into:

    2 strips, 2½" x 17½"

    2 strips, 2½" x 11½"

2 strips, 2½" x 29½"

From the brown tone on tone, cut:

3 strips, 1½" x 42"; crosscut into:

    2 strips, 1½" x 27½"

    2 strips, 1½" x 13½"

Embroidering the Designs

1. Finger-press the cream-dot 10" x 12" rectangle in half widthwise and lengthwise; use the folds as a placement guide. Open the folds and place one 10" end of the rectangle right side up over the Center design on page 28, positioning the design so that

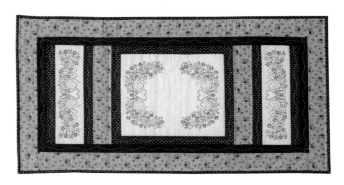

the top of the heart is 3" from the widthwise fold and the center of the heart is on the lengthwise fold. Trace the design onto the right side of the fabric. Repeat to mark the other end of the rectangle. Fuse the 10" x 12" interfacing rectangle to the wrong side of the marked rectangle.

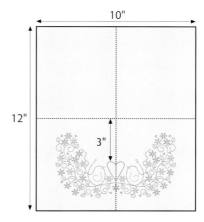

Center panel embroidery placement

2. Finger-press the 4" x 12" cream strips in half widthwise; use the fold as a placement guide. Centering the design, and with the heart on the fold, trace the Strip design on page 27 onto the right side of each strip. Fuse a 4" x 12" interfacing strip to the wrong side of each marked strip.

Strip panel embroidery placement

3. Using two strands of floss, embroider the designs, following the stitch key and color guides on the patterns.

4. Centering the embroidered design, trim the stitched rectangle to 9½" x 11½". In the same manner, trim each embroidered strip to 3½" x 11½".

Assembling the Table Runner

1. Sew a red-dot 1½" x 9½" strip to each side of the embroidered rectangle. Press the seam allowances toward the strips. Sew red-dot 1½" x 13½" strips to the top and bottom. Press the seam allowances toward the strips.

2. Sew blue-floral 2½" x 11½" strips to the top and bottom of the unit from step 1. Press the seam allowances toward the red strips. Sew red 1½" x 11½" strips to the top and bottom. Press the seam allowances toward the red strips.

3. Sew embroidered strips to the top and bottom of the unit from step 2, making sure the tops of the embroidered designs are nearest to the table-runner center. Press the seam allowances toward the red strips. Sew a red 1½" x 11½" strip to each embroidered strip. Press the seam allowances toward the red strips.

Adding the Borders

Sew a brown 1½" x 27½" strip to each long side of the table runner. Press the seam allowances toward the border. Sew a brown 1½" x 13½" strip to each short side. Press the seam allowances toward the border. Sew a blue 2½" x 29½" strip to each long side; press the seam allowances toward the inner border. Sew a blue 2½" x 17½" strip to each short side; press the seam allowances toward the inner border.

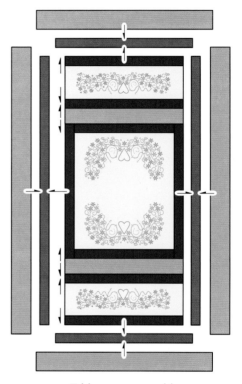

Table-runner assembly

Finishing the Table Runner

1. Layer the table-runner top, batting, and backing; baste. Use pearl cotton and big-stitch quilting (see page 10) to quilt a wavy line in each red border strip and in each brown border strip. Quilt ¼" from each blue center strip and the borders, using the quilter's tape as a guide. Trim the batting and backing even with the table-runner top.

2. Using the red 42"-long strips, make and attach the binding *before* completing the quilting next to the binding seam.

Lovebirds Table Runner

Embroidery Key

⊂ Lazy daisy

• French knot

✕✕ Cross-stitch

⎯ Backstitch

Strip design

Center design

Lovebirds Table Runner

Embroidery Key
⬭ Lazy daisy
• French knot
✕✕ Cross-stitch
—— Backstitch

little blue house wall hanging

Lovely variegated blue thread brings extra charm
to this mini bluework sampler.

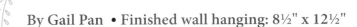

By Gail Pan • Finished wall hanging: 8½" x 12½"

Materials

Yardage is based on 42"-wide fabric.

⅛ yard of blue floral for border

⅛ yard of blue solid for binding

1 rectangle, 6" x 10", of cream handkerchief linen (see page 9) for embroidery background

10" x 14" piece of fabric for backing

10" x 14" piece of batting

1 rectangle, 6" x 10", of sheer fusible interfacing for embroidery backing

6-strand embroidery floss in variegated blue

Ecru pearl cotton, size 8

¼" quilter's tape (optional, see page 10)

Cutting

From the blue floral, cut:

1 strip, 2" x 42"; crosscut into:
  2 strips, 2" x 9½"
  2 strips, 2" x 8½"

From the blue solid, cut:

2 strips, 1½" x 42"

Embroidering the Design

1. Using the pattern on page 31, trace the Little Blue House design onto the right side of the cream linen rectangle. Fuse the interfacing rectangle to the back of the marked rectangle.

2. Using two strands of floss, embroider the design, following the stitch key on the pattern.

Finding Just the Right Hue

If you find that the color bands in the floss run longer than you'd like, or if there's a hue that you don't fancy, fussy cut the thread to stitch only with the lengths you like.

Making the Wall-Hanging Top

Centering the design, trim the stitched rectangle to 5½" x 9½". Sew the blue-floral 2" x 9½" strips to the sides of the stitched rectangle. Press the seam allowances toward the strips. Sew the blue-floral 2" x 8½" strips to the top and bottom of the rectangle. Press the seam allowances toward the strips.

Wall-hanging assembly

Finishing the Wall Hanging

1. Layer the wall-hanging top, batting, and backing; baste. Use pearl cotton and big-stitch quilting (see page 10) to quilt ¼" from each side of the seam line, using the quilter's tape as a guide.

2. Trim the batting and backing even with the top.

3. To make an optional hanging sleeve prior to binding, fold the short ends of a 4" x 6" rectangle under

¼" twice and topstitch to hem. Fold the strip in half lengthwise, *wrong* sides together, and press. Aligning the raw edges, stitch the folded strip to the top of the wall-hanging back, ⅛" from the raw edges.

4. Using the blue 1½" x 42" strips, make and attach the binding using the single-fold method *before* completing the quilting ¼" from the binding seam (do not quilt through the sleeve, if there is one). Stitch the lower (folded) edge of the sleeve to the backing by hand.

Little Blue House Wall Hanging

Embroidery Key

- Lazy daisy
- French knot
- Cross-stitch
- Satin stitch
- Running stitch
- Backstitch

bless my garden wall quilt

This redwork project features 12 designs celebrating the garden. Stitch a bird, a butterfly, and some buzzing bees to bring the garden alive.

Materials

Yardage is based on 42"-wide fabric unless otherwise noted.

1⅛ yards of red dot for blocks, border, and binding

⅜ yard of cream dot for embroidery background

⅓ yard of cream floral for sashing

⅛ yard of blue tone on tone for cornerstones

1 yard of fabric for backing

30" x 36" piece of batting

⅔ yard of lightweight fusible interfacing, 18" to 20" wide, for embroidery backing

6-strand embroidery floss in dark red

Ecru pearl cotton, size 8

Appliqué basting glue

Cutting

From the cream dot, cut:
2 strips, 5" x 42"; crosscut into 12 squares, 5" x 5"

From the lightweight fusible interfacing, cut:
12 squares, 5" x 5"

From the red dot, cut:
2 strips, 5½" x 42"; crosscut into 12 squares, 5½" x 5½"
4 strips, 3½" x 25½"
3 strips, 2½" x 42"

From the cream floral, cut:
5 strips, 1½" x 42"; crosscut into 31 strips, 1½" x 5½"

From the blue tone on tone, cut:
1 strip, 1½" x 42"; crosscut into 20 squares, 1½" x 1½"

Embroidering the Circles

1. Using the patterns on pages 35–38, trace a different Bless My Garden design onto the right side of each cream square. Trace the circles also; these are your appliqué lines. Fuse a square of interfacing to the back of each marked square.

2. Using two strands of floss, embroider the designs, following the stitch key on the patterns. Note that the outline of the small hearts is backstitched first, and then the hearts are filled in with satin stitch.

Appliquéing the Circles

1. Cut out the embroidered circles ¼" beyond the marked appliqué lines to create a ¼" turn-under allowance on each.

2. Being sure that the design is upright, glue baste an embroidered circle to the center of a red-dot 5½" square by applying two pinhead-sized dots of appliqué glue about an inch apart near the middle of the circle. Using needle-turn appliqué, stitch the circle in place, turning the edge under just until appliqué lines are no longer visible to complete the block. Repeat to make a total of 12 blocks.

Assembling the Quilt

1. To make the sashing rows, alternately join four blue tone-on-tone 1½" squares and three cream-floral 1½" x 5½" sashing strips. Repeat to make a total of five rows. Press the seam allowances toward the sashing strips.

2. Alternately join four cream-floral 1½" x 5½" sashing strips and three blocks to make a block row. Repeat to make a total of four rows. Press the seam allowances toward the sashing strips.

3. Refer to the quilt assembly diagram at right to alternately sew the sashing and block rows together. Press the seam allowances toward the sashing rows.

4. Sew two red-dot 3½" x 25½" strips to the sides of the quilt top. Press the seam allowances toward the border. Sew the remaining red-dot 3½" x 25½" strips to the top and bottom of the quilt top, and press the seam allowances toward the border.

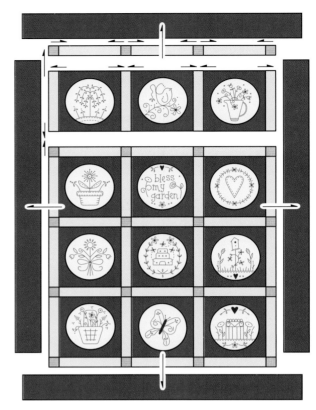

Quilt assembly

Finishing the Quilt

1. Layer the quilt top, batting, and backing; baste. Use pearl cotton and big-stitch quilting (see page 10) to quilt ¼" outside of each circle. In the border, quilt ¼" from the seam. Trim the batting and backing even with the quilt top.

2. To make an optional hanging sleeve prior to binding, fold the ends of a 5" x 22" strip under ¼" twice and topstitch to hem. Fold the strip in half lengthwise, *wrong* sides together, and press. Aligning the raw edges, stitch the folded strip to the top of the wall-hanging back, ⅛" from the raw edges.

3. Using the red-dot 2½"-wide strips, make and attach the binding *before* completing the quilting next to the binding seam (do not quilt through the sleeve if there is one). Stitch the lower (folded) edge of the sleeve to the backing.

Satin
stitch

Satin
stitch

Bless My Garden Wall Quilt

Embroidery Key

⬯ Lazy daisy

● French knot

✗✗ Cross-stitch

▨ Satin stitch

--- Running stitch

— Backstitch

Satin
stitch

Satin
stitch

Bless My Garden Wall Quilt

Embroidery Key

⌒ Lazy daisy

● French knot

✕✕ Cross-stitch

▨ Satin stitch

– – – Running stitch

——— Backstitch

Satin
stitch

Satin stitch

bless
my
garden

Satin stitch

Bless My Garden Wall Quilt

Embroidery Key

◯ Lazy daisy

● French knot

✕ ✕ Cross-stitch

▨ Satin stitch

- - - Running stitch

—— Backstitch

Satin stitch

Satin stitch

Satin stitch

Satin stitch

Bless My Garden Wall Quilt

Embroidery Key

⬭ Lazy daisy

● French knot

✕✕ Cross-stitch

▦ Satin stitch

– – – Running stitch

—— Backstitch

▬▬▬ Chainstitch

garden delight needle book

This delicate little needle book is stitched with
a delightful garden of flowers.

By Gail Pan • Finished needle book: 4" x 6½" • Finished block: 4" x 4"

Materials

Fat eighths measure 9" x 21".

1 fat eighth of red print for cover and pocket

1 piece, 5" x 21", of green print for cover and lining

1 piece, 5" x 21", of blue print for back and binding

1 piece, 5" x 7", of cream felted wool for center

1 square, 5" x 5", of cream floral for embroidery background

7" x 9" piece of batting

1 square, 5" x 5", of lightweight fusible interfacing for embroidery backing

16" length of ¼"-wide cream ribbon

9" length of ¼"-wide cream rickrack

3 cream buttons, ½" in diameter

6-strand embroidery floss in green, red, yellow, and blue

Ecru pearl cotton, size 8

Cutting

From the red print, cut:
1 rectangle, 6½" x 8½"
8 squares, 2" x 2"

From the blue print, cut:
1 square, 4½" x 4½"
2 strips, 1½" x 9"

From the green print, cut:
1 rectangle, 6½" x 8½"
1 strip, 2" x 8½"

Embroidering the Design

1. Using the pattern on page 42, trace the Garden Delight design onto the right side of the cream-floral square. Fuse the interfacing to the wrong side of the square.

2. Using two strands of floss, embroider the design, following the stitch key and color guides on the pattern.

Making the Blocks

1. Trim the embroidered square to 4½" x 4½", centering the design.

2. Mark a diagonal line on the *wrong* side of each red 2" square. Aligning the corners, pin a marked square to the embroidered square, right sides together. Sew directly on the marked line. Trim ¼" outside the seam line and press the seam allowances toward the red print. Repeat on all four corners of the embroidered square to make an embroidered Snowball block. Repeat with the remaining marked red squares and the blue-print 4½" square to make a second Snowball block.

Make 2.

Making the Needle-Book Cover

1. Lay out the two Snowball blocks and the green 2" x 8½" strip as shown. Join the Snowball blocks first and press the seam allowances open to reduce bulk. Stitch the green strip to the bottom to complete the needle-book cover. Press the seam allowances toward the strip.

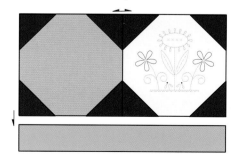

2. Sew the rickrack on top of the seam.

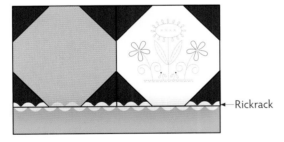

Rickrack

3. Layer the cover and the batting. Use the pearl cotton and big-stitch quilting (see page 10) to quilt ¼" from the seam lines in the Snowball blocks. Center the buttons beneath the embroidered square and sew them in place on the green strip. Trim the batting even with the cover.

Assembling the Needle Book

1. To form the pocket, fold the red rectangle in half lengthwise with *wrong* sides together to make a 3¼" x 8½" folded strip. Topstitch ⅛" from the folded edge. With a green 6½" rectangle right side

up and aligning raw edges, position the strip on one long edge of the rectangle and baste it in place to make the lining.

2. Cut the cream ribbon in half. With the lining right side up and with the pocket at the bottom, place the two lengths of ribbon so that one end of each length is centered on a side (shorter) edge of the lining and overhangs the edge by approximately ¼". Pin the ends in place. The remainder of the ribbon should be lying completely on the lining, with only the overhanging end of each length in the seam allowance.

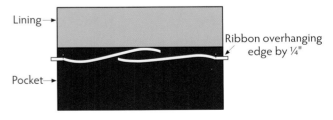

Lining→

Ribbon overhanging edge by ¼"

Pocket→

3. Place the cover on the lining, right side down, and pin together along the sides. Sew the side seams only, catching the ribbons in the seams as you sew.

Finishing the Needle Book

Turn the needle book right side out and press. Use the two blue strips to make single-fold binding and attach it to the top and bottom edges. Center the wool rectangle on the inside of the needle book and backstitch through the center to form pages for your needles.

French knots

Garden Delight Needle Book

Embroidery Key
⬭ Lazy daisy
● French knot
♣ Fill in with French knots
✕✕ Cross-stitch
– – – Running stitch
—— Backstitch

secrets and dreams folder

This embroidered journal cover, pattern holder, or secret keeper is just the right place to store those special dreams, plans, or souvenirs.

By Gail Pan • Finished folder: 4" x 6"

Materials

Yardage is based on 42"-wide fabric. Fat quarters measure 18" x 21".

⅜ yard of purple print for front, pocket, and back
⅓ yard of blue print for front, pocket, and binding
¼ yard of green print for front and pocket
1 fat quarter of blue-and-cream print for pocket
1 rectangle, 6" x 8", of cream dot for embroidery
   background
1 piece, 5" x 9", of red print for cover
11" x 15" piece of batting
1 rectangle, 6" x 8", of lightweight fusible interfacing
   for embroidery backing
6-strand embroidery floss in red, yellow, purple,
   dark green, green, and dark blue
Ecru pearl cotton, size 8
¼" quilter's tape (optional, see page 10)
1 thin elastic ponytail holder
1 cream button, ¾" in diameter

Cutting

From the green print, cut:
2 rectangles, 6½" x 10½"
1 strip, 1½" x 8½"

From the blue print, cut:
1 strip, 1½" x 42", crosscut into:
   2 strips, 1½" x 15½"
   1 strip, 1½" x 5½"
1 rectangle, 6½" x 14"

From the purple print, cut:
1 strip, 10½" x 42"; crosscut into:
   1 rectangle, 10½" x 14½"
   1 rectangle, 7½" x 10½"
   1 rectangle, 6½" x 10"
1 strip, 1½" x 8½"

From the blue-and-cream print, cut:
1 rectangle, 10½" x 12½"

From the red print, cut:
2 strips, 1½" x 7½"

Embroidering the Design

1. Using the pattern on page 47, trace the Secrets and Dreams design onto the right side of the cream-dot rectangle. Fuse the interfacing rectangle to the wrong side of the marked rectangle.

2. Using two strands of floss, embroider the design, following the stitch key and color guides on the pattern.

Making the Folder Cover

1. Centering the embroidery, trim the stitched rectangle to 5½" x 7½".

2. Sew the blue 1½" x 5½" strip to the bottom of the trimmed rectangle. Press the seam allowances toward the strip. Sew the green 1½" x 8½" strip to the left side of the rectangle and the purple

1½" x 8½" strip to the right side of the rectangle. Press the seam allowances toward the strips. Add the red 1½" x 7½" strips to the top and bottom to complete the pieced rectangle for the front of the folder. Press the seam allowances toward the strips. With right sides together, sew the purple 7½" x 10½" rectangle to the left edge of the folder front to make the back of the folder. Press the seam allowances toward the purple fabric to complete the folder cover.

Quilting the Folder Cover

Layer the cover and the batting. Use the pearl cotton and big-stitch quilting (see page 10) to quilt a wavy frame around the embroidery, a wavy line in the center of the blue strip, and three equally spaced, parallel wavy lines down the back. Quilt ¼" from the seam in the green, purple, and red strips. Trim the batting even with the fabric.

Making the Folder Pockets

1. To make the folder pockets, fold the blue 6½" x 14" rectangle in half, wrong sides together, to make a 6½" x 7" folded rectangle. Press, and then topstitch along the fold. Fold the purple 6½" x 10" rectangle in half, wrong sides together, to make a 5" x 6½" folded rectangle. Press, and then topstitch along the fold.

2. Aligning raw edges at the sides and bottom, layer the purple pocket on the blue pocket. Place the layered pockets on a green 6½" x 10½" rectangle, right side up, with side and bottom edges aligned. Baste the pockets in place, ⅛" from the raw edges.

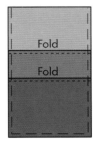

Baste.

3. Place the second green rectangle right side down on the first, aligning raw edges. Stitch the rectangles together on the right edge.

4. Fold the second green rectangle to the back, press, and then topstitch along the fold to complete the pocket rectangle.

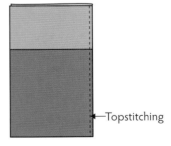

Topstitching

5. Place the pocket rectangle, pocket side up, on the left side of the purple 10½" x 14½" lining rectangle, right side up. Align raw edges at the

top, bottom, and left sides. Baste ⅛" from the raw edges through all layers. To make the right side pocket, fold the blue-and-cream rectangle in half, wrong sides together, to make a 6¼" x 10½" folded rectangle. Press, and then topstitch along the fold. Aligning raw edges, place this pocket on the right-hand side of the purple lining rectangle. Baste ⅛" from the raw edges through all layers.

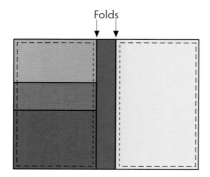

Folds

Baste raw edges.

Assembling the Folder

1. Pinch the ponytail holder to form a 1" loop, and then wrap thread around the pinched elastic to hold the 1" loop in place. Machine stitch across the wrapped thread to secure, and then trim the excess elastic ¼" from the stitching.

1"   Trim.

2. Position the loop on the right edge of the blue-and-cream pocket, centered between the top and bottom edges, and with the cut ends of the loop

overhanging the edge. The loop should be lying on the blue-and-cream pocket. Baste or pin in place.

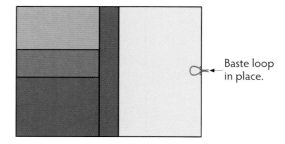

Baste loop in place.

3. Making sure that the top of the quilted cover is aligned with the top of the pocketed lining, place the cover right side down on the lining. Sew the side seams only, catching the ponytail holder in the seam.

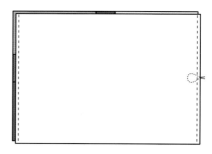

4. Turn the folder right side out and press well. Sew a vertical line through the center of the folder to secure the layers. Use the two blue 15½"-long strips to make single-fold binding and attach it to the top and bottom edges. Sew the button in place on the front of the folder, ½" in from the right edge, centered between the top and bottom edges, and aligned with the loop. Slip the loop over the button to hold the folder closed.

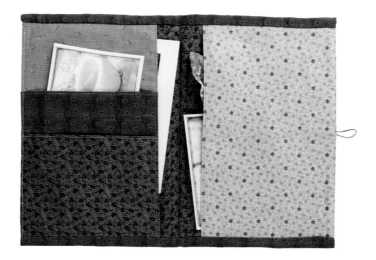

French knots

Secrets and Dreams Folder

Embroidery Key

⬭ Lazy daisy

● French knot

– – – Running stitch

—— Backstitch

home pillow

This homey redwork pillow is just right
for country decorating.

By Gail Pan • Finished pillow: 16" x 16" • Finished block: 6" x 8"

Materials

Yardage is based on 42"-wide fabric. Fat quarters measure 18" x 21".

¼ yard of red vine print for pillow front

⅛ yard of cream-and-red floral for pillow front

1 rectangle, 8" x 10", of cream solid for embroidery background

1 rectangle, 2½" x 5" *each*, of 4 assorted red prints for squares

1 fat quarter of fabric for pillow back

1 rectangle, 8" x 10", of lightweight fusible interfacing for embroidery backing

Variegated dark-red pearl cotton, size 12

Ecru pearl cotton, size 8

4 cream buttons, ½" in diameter

18" x 18" piece of batting

16" x 16" pillow form

¼" quilter's tape (optional, see page 10)

Cutting

From *each* of the assorted red prints, cut:

2 squares, 2½" x 2½"

From the red vine print, cut:

3 strips, 1½" x 42"; crosscut into:

    2 strips, 1½" x 8½"

    2 strips, 1½" x 10½"

    2 strips, 1½" x 14½"

    2 strips, 1½" x 16½"

From the cream-and-red floral, cut:

1 strip, 2½" x 42"; crosscut into 4 strips, 2½" x 10½"

From the backing fabric, cut:

2 rectangles, 8½" x 16½"

Embroidering the Design

1. Using the pattern on page 51, trace the Home design onto the right side of the cream-solid rectangle. Fuse the interfacing rectangle to the wrong side of the marked rectangle.

2. Using one strand of dark-red pearl cotton, embroider the design, following the stitch key on the pattern.

Making the Pillow Top

1. Centering the design, trim the embroidered rectangle to 6½" x 8½". Join four different red 2½" squares into a strip. Press the seam allowances in one direction.

2. Sew the strip to the bottom edge of the embroidered rectangle. Press the seam allowances toward the rectangle. Sew the two red vine-print 1½" x 8½" strips to the sides. Press the seam

allowances toward the strips. Sew the two red vine-print 1½" x 10½" strips to the top and bottom. Press the seam allowances toward the strips.

3. Sew two cream-and-red 2½" x 10½" strips to the sides of the pillow top. Press the seam allowances toward the red strips. Sew an assorted red 2½" square to each end of the remaining cream-and-red 2½" x 10½" strips. Press the seam allowances toward the red squares. Sew the strips to the top and bottom of the pillow top. Press the seam allowances toward the red strips.

4. Sew the red vine-print 1½" x 14½" strips to the sides of the pillow top. Press the seam allowances toward the red strips. Sew the red vine-print 1½" x 16½" strips to the top and bottom. Press the seam allowances toward the red strips.

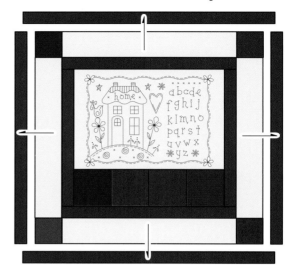

Finishing the Pillow

1. Using a ¼" seam allowance and with *right* sides facing, sew the two backing rectangles together along one long edge, leaving a 10"-wide opening in the center of the seam for turning and for inserting the pillow form. Press the seam allowances to one side.

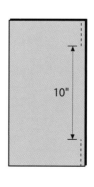

Backing

2. Baste the pillow top to the batting square. Using pearl cotton and big-stitch quilting (see page 10), quilt an X in each red square, and then quilt ¼" from the seams in the red strips. Quilt a wavy line through the center of each cream-and-red strip. Trim the batting even with the pillow top. Sew a button in the center of each red square below the house block.

3. Aligning the raw edges, and with right sides together, pin the pillow top to the pieced backing. Sew ¼" from the raw edges all the way around, pivoting at the corners.

4. Trim the corners. Turn the pillow cover right side out and press. Insert the 16" pillow form and slip-stitch the opening closed.

Embroidery Key

⌒ Lazy daisy

• French knot

✕✕ Cross-stitch

▨ Satin stitch

– – – Running stitch

—— Backstitch

Satin stitch

Home Pillow

pincushion collection

These three cute pincushions, embellished with buttons, lace, and rickrack, are sure to delight. Use them to add charm to any room, or put them to work in your sewing space, storing a different type of pin on each one.

Materials

Fat eighths measure 9" x 21". Materials are sufficient to make all 3 pincushions.

1 fat eighth of cream dot for embroidery backgrounds

1 piece, 6" x 11" *each*, of 2 different red prints for piecing and backing of House and Bloom pincushions

1 piece, 6" x 11", of blue print for piecing and backing of Bird pincushion

1 fat eighth of lightweight fusible interfacing for embroidery backing

Assorted pieces of lace and/or rickrack, ¼" to ⅜" wide, and each at least each 6" long

6 off-white buttons, ½" in diameter

6-strand embroidery floss in red, blue, pink, light green, dark green, and yellow

Fiberfill and/or ground walnut shells for stuffing (see "Why Walnut Shells?" on page 18)

Cutting

From the cream dot, cut:

3 squares, 5" x 5"

From the lightweight fusible interfacing, cut:

3 squares, 5" x 5"

From *each* of the red prints, cut:

1 rectangle, 2½" x 4½"

2 rectangles, 3½" x 4½"

From the blue print, cut:

1 rectangle, 2½" x 4½"

2 rectangles, 3½" x 4½"

Embroidering the Designs

1. Using the patterns on page 55, trace each pincushion design onto the right side of a cream-dot square. Fuse each interfacing square to the wrong side of a marked square.

2. Using two strands of floss, embroider the designs, following the stitch keys and color guides on the patterns.

Making the Pincushions

HOUSE PINCUSHION

1. Centering the embroidery, trim the embroidered House square to 4½" x 4½". Select a set of three matching red-print rectangles. Sew a red 2½" x 4½" rectangle to the bottom of the House square. Press the seam allowances toward the red print. Stitch a piece of lace on top of the seam. Evenly space three buttons below the house and sew them in place.

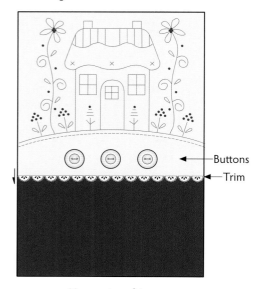

House pincushion

2. Using a ¼" seam allowance and with right sides together, sew two 3½" x 4½" rectangles along one long edge to make the backing, leaving a 1½"-wide opening in the center of the seam for turning. Press the seam allowances to one side.

3. Aligning the raw edges, and with right sides together, pin the pincushion top to the pieced backing. Sew ¼" from the raw edges all the way around, pivoting at the corners.

4. Trim the corners. Turn the pincushion right side out through the opening and press. Stuff firmly with fiberfill and/or walnut shells. Hand stitch the opening closed.

BIRD PINCUSHION

Make as for the House pincushion, using the blue set of rectangles, adding rickrack in place of the lace, and sewing the buttons to the blue rectangle instead of to the embroidered square.

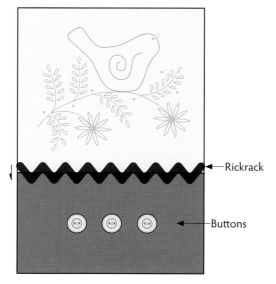

Bird pincushion

BLOOM PINCUSHION

Make as for the House pincushion, using the other set of red rectangles and sewing the 2½" x 4½" red rectangle to the left side of the embroidered square rather than to the bottom. Stitch lace on top of the seam.

Bloom pincushion

French knots

French knots

French knots

bloom

Pincushion Collection

Embroidery Key

⌒ Lazy daisy

● French knot

✗✗ Cross-stitch

♣ Fill in with French knots

– – – Running stitch

—— Backstitch

happily ever after sewing bag

This medium-sized sewing bag twinkles with redwork, buttons, and big-stitch quilting and is large enough to hold your current embroidery project, plus pattern, threads, needles, pins, and scissors!

Materials

Yardage is based on 42"-wide fabric unless otherwise noted. Fat quarters measure 18" x 21".

½ yard of blue print for bag, handles, and drawstrings

½ yard of tan shirting print for top of bag

1 fat quarter of beige print for lining

⅛ yard of red stripe for casings and binding

1 rectangle, 7" x 9", of beige solid for embroidery background

2 pieces of batting, 9" x 13" *each*

1 rectangle, 7" x 9", of lightweight fusible interfacing for embroidery backing

8 cream buttons, ½" in diameter

2 skeins of 6-strand embroidery floss in variegated reddish brown

Ecru pearl cotton, size 8

¼" quilter's tape (optional, see page 10)

Appliqué basting glue

Cutting

From the blue print, cut:
2 rectangles, 8½" x 12½"
2 strips, 2" x 32"
2 strips, 1½" x 30"

From the tan shirting print, cut:
2 rectangles, 12½" x 16"

From the red stripe, cut:
1 strip, 1½" x 24½"
2 strips, 1½" x 9½"

From the beige print, cut:
2 rectangles, 8" x 12"

Embroidering the Design

1. Using the pattern on page 60, trace the Happily Ever After design onto the right side of the beige-solid rectangle. Trace the oval also; this is your appliqué line. Fuse the interfacing rectangle to the back of the marked rectangle.

2. Using two strands of floss, embroider the design, following the stitch key and color guides on the pattern.

Appliquéing the Oval

1. Cut out the embroidered oval ¼" beyond the marked appliqué line to create a ¼" turn-under allowance.

2. With the design upright, center the oval on the right side of a blue-print 8½" x 12½" rectangle. Glue baste the oval in place by applying several pinhead-sized dots of appliqué glue about an inch apart near the middle of the oval. Using needle-turn appliqué, stitch the oval in place, turning the edge under just until the appliqué line is no longer visible.

Making the Bag

1. Baste the appliquéd rectangle to a batting rectangle to make the bag front. Using pearl cotton and big-stitch quilting (see page 10), quilt the bag front ¼" beyond the appliquéd oval. Trim the batting even with the fabric. Baste the remaining blue rectangle to the remaining batting rectangle to make the bag back. Trim the batting even with the fabric.

2. Place the front and back rectangles right sides together and, using a ¼" seam allowance, sew down one side of the bag, across the bottom, and up the other side. With the bag still wrong side out, box one bottom corner by bringing the bottom seam together with a side seam. Press flat

and pin. Measure 2" from the corner and draw a line perpendicular to the seams. Sew along this line, and then trim ¼" from the stitching line. Repeat for the other corner.

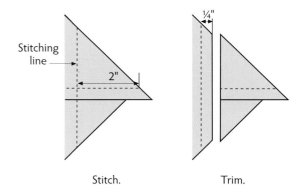

Stitching line

2"

¼"

Stitch.   Trim.

3. Repeat step 2 using the two beige-print lining rectangles.

4. Place the lining inside the bag, *wrong* sides together, and baste together ⅛" from the top edge.

5. Aligning the raw edges, pin the two shirting rectangles right sides together and sew a ¼" seam along each 16" edge to make a tube 12" wide and 16" tall. Press the seam allowances open. Fold the tube down on itself, *wrong* sides together, to make a tube that measures 12" wide and 8" tall. Top-stitch along the folded edge. This will be the top edge of the bag.

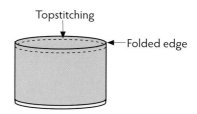

Topstitching

Folded edge

6. To make a casing, fold under ¼" on both short ends of a red-stripe 1½" x 9½" strip. Press, and then topstitch along the folds. Fold under ¼" on both long edges of the strip and press. Repeat to make the second casing.

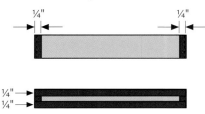

7. Position the casings on the front and the back of the shirting tube, ¾" from the top of the tube and an equal distance from each side seam. Pin in place. Backstitching at each end of the stitching line to secure, topstitch the long edges of one casing to the folded tube, leaving the casing ends open. Repeat with the second casing. Pull the threads to the inside of the tube and tie them off. Trim the threads.

8. Sew two blue-print 2" x 32" strips right sides together along both long edges. Turn right side out and press. Topstitch along each long edge. Cut into two equal lengths to make the handles. Position one handle on the front of the bag so that each handle end is 3¼" from a side seam. Aligning the raw edges of the ends with the basted top of the bag, pin the handle ends in place, being careful not to twist the handle. Repeat with the second handle on the back of the bag.

9. Place the shirting tube inside the bag, top edge down, casings visible at the center of the bag, and with raw edges aligned. Using a ¼" seam allowance, stitch the tube and the bag together along the raw edges. With the tube still inside the bag, use the red-stripe 1½" x 24½" strip to bind the raw edges with single-fold binding. Pull the shirting tube out of the bag and press along the binding.

Finishing the Bag

1. To make the drawstrings, press under ¼" on each end of a blue-print 1½" x 30" strip. Fold the strip in half lengthwise, wrong sides together, and press to form a crease. Open the strip, and then fold each long raw edge of the strip to the crease. Fold again, enclosing the raw edges, and press. Topstitch down each long side and across both ends. Repeat to make the second drawstring.

2. Thread one of the drawstrings through one casing and around and through the other. Making sure the drawstring isn't twisted, position one end on top of the other with ends and edges aligned. Sew across the drawstring several times through all layers, approximately 1" from the ends. Sew a button to the outside of each end. Starting at the opposite side of the bag, thread the second drawstring through the casings. Finish the second drawstring in the same manner as the first. Pull the drawstrings to close the bag.

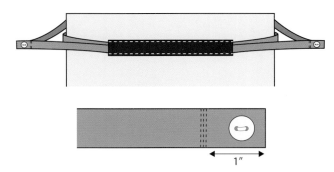

French
knot

Happily Ever After Sewing Bag

Embroidery Key

⬯ Lazy daisy

● French knot

✕✕ Cross-stitch

– – – Running stitch

——— Backstitch

flower baskets lap quilt

Two dozen embroidered flower baskets adorn this cozy lap quilt, perfect for snuggling under on the couch.

Designed and embroidered by Gail Pan • Pieced and bound by Sandra McLay
Machine quilted by Hermione Agee • Finished quilt: 50½" x 57½" • Finished block: 6" x 7"

Materials

Yardage is based on 42"-wide fabric unless otherwise noted.

1⅝ yards of red dot for border and binding

⅔ yard of cream dot for embroidery backgrounds

⅓ yard *each* of 11 assorted prints for blocks

⅓ yard of red-and-gold print for blocks

3⅜ yards of fabric for backing (horizontal seam)

55" x 62" piece of batting

1½ yards of lightweight fusible interfacing, 18" to 20" wide, for embroidery backings

6-strand variegated embroidery floss: 4 skeins of brown; 1 skein each of dark green, burgundy, light blue, medium green, teal, light green, light pink, bluish green, celery, sky blue, teal, light mauve, pinkish purple, light pink, light gold, orange, orangish red.

Cutting

From the cream dot, cut:

4 strips, 5" x 42"; crosscut into 24 rectangles, 5" x 6"

From the lightweight fusible interfacing, cut:

8 strips, 6" x 18" to 20"; crosscut into 24 rectangles, 5" x 6"

From *each* of the 11 assorted prints, cut:

1 strip, 5½" x 42"; crosscut into:
  2 rectangles, 4½" x 5½" (22 total)
  8 strips, 1½" x 5½" (88 total)

2 strips, 1½" x 42"; crosscut into 8 strips, 1½" x 6½" (88 total)

From the red-and-gold print, cut;

1 strip, 5½" x 42"; crosscut into:
  3 rectangles, 4½" x 5½"
  10 strips, 1½" x 5½"

2 strips, 1½" x 42"; crosscut into 10 strips, 1½" x 6½"

From the *lengthwise* grain of the red dot, cut:

2 strips, 4½" x 49½"

2 strips, 4½" x 50½"

5 strips, 2½" x 50"

Embroidering the Designs

1. Using the patterns on page 65, first center and trace the Basket design onto the right side of all 24 cream-dot rectangles, and then trace the eight Flower designs, three times *each*, inside an already-traced basket on a cream rectangle. Fuse an interfacing rectangle to the wrong side of each marked rectangle.

2. Using two strands of floss, embroider the designs, following the stitch key and color guides on the patterns.

Making the Blocks

1. Each block, with or without an embroidered center, uses four matching-print strips: two that are 1½" x 5½" and two that are 1½" x 6½". Centering the embroidery, trim each embroidered rectangle to 4½" x 5½". Sew two 1½" x 5½" strips to the sides of an embroidered rectangle. Press the seam allowances toward the strips. Sew two matching 1½" x 6½" strips to the top and bottom of the rectangle. Press the seam allowances toward the strips to complete one embroidered block. Make 24 embroidered blocks.

Make 24.

2. Sew two 1½" x 5½" strips to the sides of one assorted-print 4½" x 5½" rectangle. Press the seam allowances toward the strips. Sew two matching 1½" x 6½" strips to the top and bottom of the rectangle. Press the seam allowances toward the strips to complete one plain block. Make 25 plain blocks.

 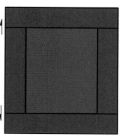

Make 25.

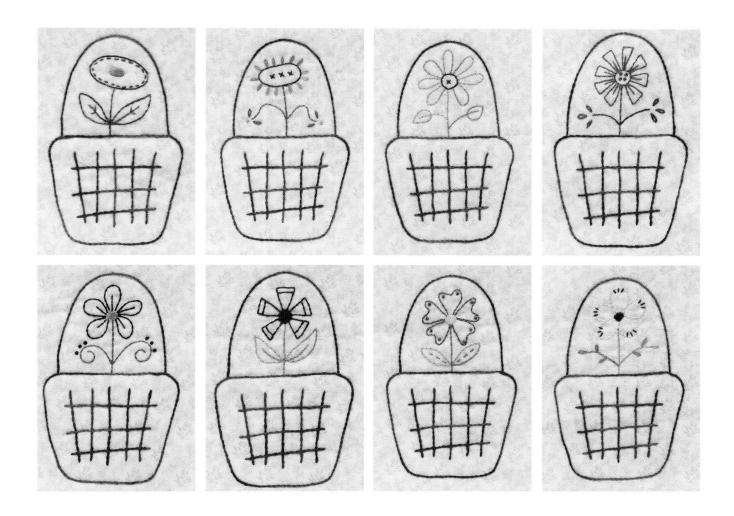

Assembling the Quilt

1. Arrange the plain and embroidered blocks into seven horizontal rows of seven blocks each, alternating them as shown. Sew the blocks together into rows. Press the seam allowances in opposite directions from row to row. Sew the rows together to complete the quilt center; press the seam allowances in one direction.

2. Sew the red-dot 49½"-long strips to the sides of the quilt. Press the seam allowances toward the strips. Sew the red-dot 50½"-long strips to the top and bottom of the quilt. Press the seam allowances toward the strips.

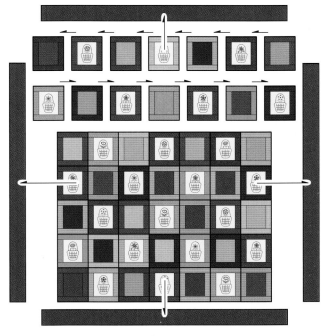

Quilt assembly

Finishing the Quilt

1. Layer the quilt top, batting, and backing; baste the layers together. Quilt as desired. Hermione machine quilted a wavy frame in the strips surrounding each rectangle. She quilted double swags in the border, with each swag corresponding to a block. The border corners are quilted with an oval formed of double curved lines.

2. Trim the batting and backing even with the quilt top. Using the red-dot 2½" x 50" strips, make and attach the double-fold binding.

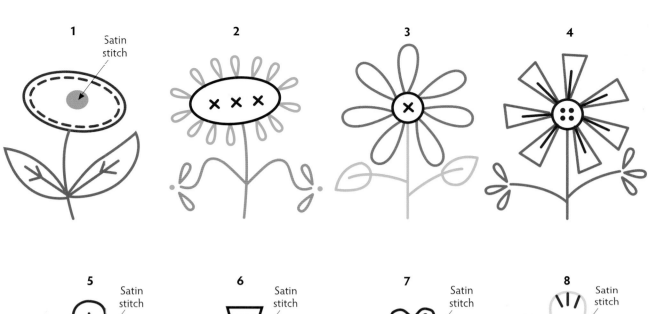

1 Satin stitch

2

3

4

5 Satin stitch

6 Satin stitch

7 Satin stitch

8 Satin stitch

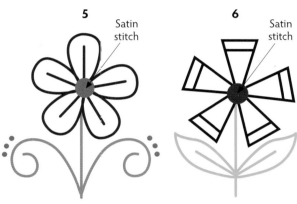

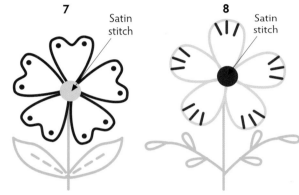

Flower Baskets Lap Quilt

Embroidery Key

⬯ Lazy daisy

• French knot

✕✕ Cross-stitch

– – – Running stitch

▨ Satin stitch

········· Stem stitch

——— Backstitch

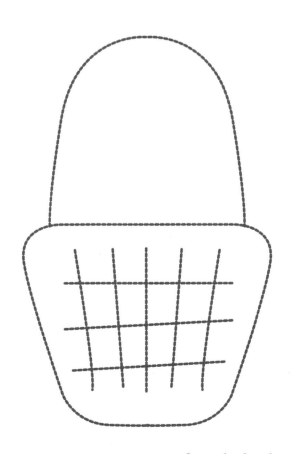

redwork tote

You're bound to smile when you see the cheerful redwork panel on the front of this charming tote bag.

Materials

Yardage is based on 42"-wide fabric unless otherwise noted.

⅝ yard of beige print for lining

⅜ yard of cream-and-red floral for bag front and back

¼ yard of red solid for bag bottom and trim

¼ yard of cream-and-red stripe for bag front, back, and handles

1 rectangle, 7" x 9", of cream handkerchief linen (see page 9) for embroidery background

2 pieces of batting, 17" x 18"

2 pieces of batting, 3" x 22"

1 rectangle, 7" x 9", of lightweight fusible interfacing for embroidery backing

6-strand embroidery floss in variegated reddish brown

Ecru pearl cotton, size 8

Appliqué basting glue

¼" quilter's tape (optional, see page 10)

Cutting

From the red solid, cut:

1 strip, 4½" x 42"; crosscut into 2 strips, 4½" x 16½"

1 strip, 1½" x 42"; crosscut into 2 strips, 1½" x 16½"

1 strip, 1" x 42"; crosscut into:
    2 strips, 1" x 6½"
    2 strips, 1" x 8½"

From the cream-and-red stripe, cut:

2 strips, 1½" x 42"; crosscut into 3 strips, 1½" x 16½"

2 strips, 2" x 42"; crosscut into 4 strips, 2" x 20"

From the cream-and-red floral, cut:

1 rectangle, 9½" x 16½"

2 rectangles, 4½" x 6½"

1 strip, 2½" x 16½"

From the beige print, cut:

2 rectangles, 15½" x 16½"

Embroidering the Design

1. Using the pattern on page 70, trace the Redwork design onto the right side of the cream linen rectangle. Fuse the interfacing rectangle to the wrong side of the marked rectangle.

2. Using two strands of floss, embroider the design, following the stitch key on the pattern.

Making the Tote Front and Back

1. Centering the embroidery, trim the embroidered panel to 6½" x 8½".

2. Fold both red-solid 1" x 6½" strips *wrong* sides together to make two strips ½" x 6½". Press. Fold both red-solid 1" x 8½" strips *wrong* sides together to make two strips ½" x 8½". Press.

3. Aligning the raw edges of the folded 6½"-long strips with the sides of the embroidered panel, glue baste the folded strips to the front of the panel by applying pinhead-sized dots ⅛" from the raw edge and an inch apart to the underside of the folded strip and gently pressing it in place. Repeat on the top and bottom of the panel using the folded 8½"-long strips.

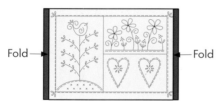

Fold → ← Fold

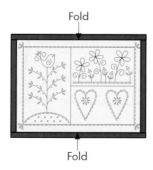

Fold

Fold

4. Sew a cream-and-red-floral 4½" x 6½" rectangle to each side of the panel to make a pieced strip. Press the seam allowances toward the floral rectangles.

5. With the floral strip in the middle, sew together a red-solid 1½" x 16½" strip, a cream-and-red-floral 2½" x 16½" strip, and a cream-and-red-stripe 1½" x 16½" strip. Press the seam allowances away from the floral strip. Sew the pieced panel strip to the striped strip. Press the seam allowances toward the striped strip. Sew a cream-and-red-stripe 16½"-long strip to the bottom of the panel strip. Press the seam allowances toward the striped strip. Add a red-solid 4½" x 16½" strip to the striped strip. Press the seam allowances toward the solid strip to complete the tote front.

6. Sew a red-solid 1½" x 16½" strip to one long edge of the cream-and-red-floral 9½" x 16½" rectangle. Press the seam allowances toward the solid strip. Sew a cream-and-red-stripe 1½" x 16½" strip to the other long edge of the floral rectangle. Press the seam allowances toward the rectangle. Sew a red-solid 4½" x 16½" rectangle to the striped strip.

Press the seam allowances toward the solid strip to complete the tote back.

Back panel

7. With right sides together, align the raw edges of two cream-and-red-stripe 2" x 20" strips. Place the aligned strips on a 3" x 22" piece of batting and pin in place. Sew the strips together along both long edges. Trim the batting even with the strips and turn right side out. Press, and then topstitch along each long edge to complete one handle. Repeat to make a second handle.

Assembling the Tote

1. Baste the front of the tote to a batting rectangle. Using the pearl cotton and big-stitch quilting (see page 10), quilt ¼" from each side of the seam lines. Trim the batting even with the tote front. Baste the tote back to a batting rectangle and quilt ¼" from each side of the seam lines. Trim the batting even with the tote back.

2. Place the back and front rectangles right sides together and pin. Using a ¼" seam allowance, sew down one side of the tote, across the bottom, and up the other side. With the tote still wrong side out, box one bottom corner by bringing the bottom seam together with a side seam. Press flat and pin. Measure 2" from the corner and draw a line perpendicular to the seams. Sew along this

line, and then trim ¼" from the stitching line. Repeat for the other corner. Turn right side out.

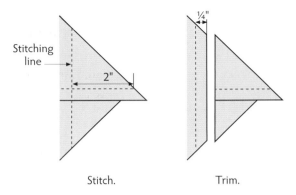

Stitch.   Trim.

3. Place the lining rectangles right sides together and pin. Leaving a 4" opening in the bottom seam for turning, sew down a 15½" side, across the bottom, and up the other 15½" side. Leave a 4" opening in the bottom seam for turning. Box the lining corners in the same way as the tote corners.

4. Position one handle on the front of the tote so that each handle end is 4½" from a side seam. Aligning the raw edges of the ends with the raw edges at the top of the tote, pin the handle ends in place, being careful not to twist the handle. Repeat with the second handle on the back of the tote.

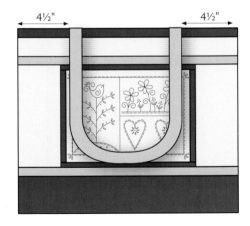

5. Aligning the raw edges at the top, place the tote inside the lining, right sides together, matching the side seams. Pin in place, and then sew around the top raw edges. Turn the tote right side out through the opening in the lining. Sew the opening in the lining closed. Push the lining into the bag and press well. Topstitch around the top of the tote, ⅛" from the top edge.

French knots

Redwork Tote

Embroidery Key

Lazy daisy

● French knot

✕✕ Cross-stitch

♣ Fill in with French knots

− − − Running stitch

—— Backstitch

stitch a little love sewing folder

Keep all of the materials for a sewing project together
and organized in this charming sewing folder.

Materials

Yardage is based on 42"-wide fabric. Fat quarters measure 18" x 21".

⅝ yard of dark-blue print for cover

1 fat quarter of light-blue print for lining and squares

1 rectangle, 7" x 11", of dark-beige solid for embroidery background

7 strips, 1½" x 11" *each*, of assorted prints

1 rectangle, 12" x 18", of batting

1 rectangle, 7" x 11", of lightweight fusible interfacing for embroidery backing

1¼ yards of cream ⅛"-diameter cord

6-strand variegated embroidery floss in red, green, blue, and gray

Ecru pearl cotton, size 8

Chalk pencil

Appliqué basting glue

¼" quilter's tape (optional, see page 10)

Cutting

From the dark-blue print, cut:

1 strip, 16½" x 42"; crosscut into:
  1 rectangle, 8½" x 16½"
  1 rectangle, 6¼" x 16½"
  1 strip, 4½" x 16½"

1 strip, 1½" x 42"; crosscut into 2 strips, 1½" x 18"

From the light-blue print, cut:

1 rectangle, 10½" x 16½"

1 strip, 1½" x 11"

Embroidering the Designs

1. Using the patterns on page 75, trace the circles for both Stitch a Little Love designs onto the right side of the dark-beige rectangle (at least ¾" apart); these are your appliqué lines. Trace the embroidery designs in the centers of the circles. Fuse the interfacing rectangle to the wrong side of the marked rectangle.

2. Using two strands of floss, embroider the designs, following the stitch key and color guides on the patterns.

Making the Folder Cover and Pocket

1. Cut out the embroidered circles ¼" beyond the marked appliqué line to create a ¼" turn-under allowance.

2. Fold the dark-blue 8½" x 16½" rectangle in half widthwise, wrong sides together, to form the cover. Allowing for the ¼" seam allowance on the right edge, center the larger circle appliqué, with design upright, onto the right half of the strip. Glue baste it in place by applying two pinhead-sized dots of appliqué glue about an inch apart near the middle of the circle. Using needle-turn appliqué, stitch the circle in place, turning the edge under just until the appliqué line is no longer visible. Repeat with the small embroidered circle and the dark-blue 4½" x 16½" strip to make the pocket strip.

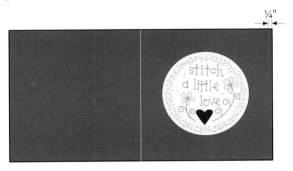

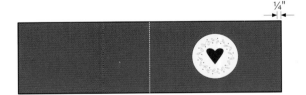

3. Sew the eight assorted 1½" x 11" strips (including the light-blue strip) together as shown. Press the seam allowances in one direction. Crosscut the strip unit into six segments, 1½" x 8½" each. Each segment will contain eight squares.

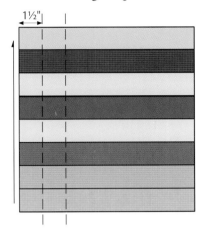

4. Sew two segments together end to end to make a pieced strip of 16 squares. Press the seam allowances in the same direction. Repeat to make two additional pieced strips of 16 squares each.

5. Sew pieced strips to the top and bottom of the appliquéd cover strip as shown. Press the seam allowances toward the cover strip.

6. Sew the remaining pieced strip to the top of the 4½" x 16½" appliquéd pocket strip. Press the seam allowances toward the pocket strip. Sew the dark-blue 6¼" x 16½" rectangle to the top of the assorted fabric strip. Press the seam allowances toward the dark-blue rectangle. Fold the dark-blue 6¼" x 16½" rectangle to the back,

leaving ¼" showing above the pieced strip. Press, and then topstitch along the fold. This is the top of the pocket.

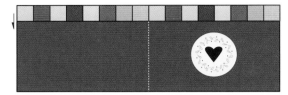

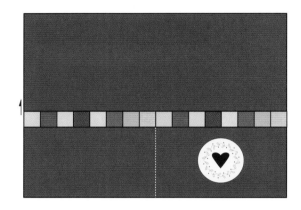

Fold

¼"

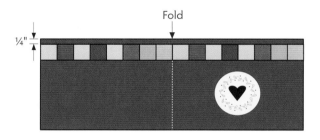

Finishing the Folder

1. Baste the cover to the batting rectangle. Using the pearl cotton and big-stitch quilting (see page 10), quilt a ring ¼" outside the appliquéd circle, two parallel lines across the pieced strips, and ¼" from the seam lines. Trim the batting even with the cover. Without using batting, quilt two parallel lines across the pieced strip on the pocket through both layers of fabric. Aligning the raw edges, place the pocket on the light-blue 10½" x 16½" lining rectangle and pin in place. Measure 4¼" from the left edge of the pocket and use a ceramic pencil

to draw a line on the pocket parallel to the edge. Backstitching to secure, sew on this line to make two smaller pockets.

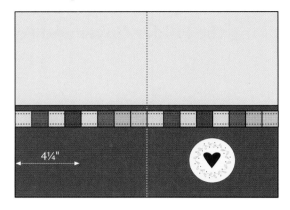

4¼"

2. Cut the cream cord in half. With the lining right side up and with the pocket at the bottom, position the two lengths of cord so that one end of each length is centered on a side edge of the lining and overhangs the edge by approximately ¼". Pin the ends in place. The remainder of the cord should be lying completely on the lining, with only the overhanging end of each length in the seam allowance.

3. Place the cover on the lining, right side down, and pin together along the sides. Sew the side seams only, catching the cord ends in the seams as you sew. Turn right side out and topstitch down each side edge. Sew a vertical line down the middle of the folder, creating one more pocket.

4. Use the dark-blue 1½" x 18" strips to make single-fold binding and attach it to the top and bottom edges of the folder.

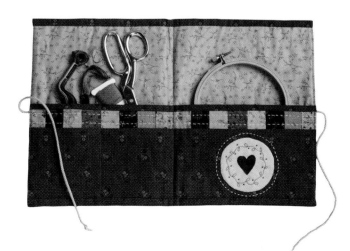

Stitch a Little Love Sewing Folder

Embroidery Key

- ⌒ Lazy daisy
- • French knot
- ▨ Satin stitch
- ----- Stem stitch
- —— Backstitch

Satin stitch

Satin stitch

garden bed table mat

Adorn your table with this cute little quilt.

Materials

Yardage is based on 42"-wide fabric unless noted otherwise. Fat eighths measure 9" x 21".

⅜ yard of beige tone on tone for embroidery backgrounds

1 fat eighth *each* of 2 blue prints, 3 green prints, and 3 red prints for squares

½ yard of small-scale blue print for squares and binding

½ yard of red print for borders

1¼ yards of fabric for backing

37" x 37" piece of batting

1⅓ yards of lightweight fusible interfacing, 18" to 20" wide, for embroidery backings

6-strand variegated embroidery floss in pine green, moss green, mint green, light pink, dark red, and blue

Ecru pearl cotton, size 8

¼" quilter's tape (optional, see page 10)

Cutting

From the beige tone on tone, cut:
2 strips, 5" x 42"; crosscut into 4 strips, 5" x 21"

From the lightweight fusible interfacing, cut:
4 strips, 5" x 21"

From 1 of the blue fat eighths, cut:
1 square, 4½" x 4½"
4 squares, 3½" x 3½"

From *each* of 2 of the green fat eighths, cut:
1 square, 4½" x 4½"
4 squares, 3½" x 3½"

From *each* of the 5 remaining fat eighths, cut:
4 squares, 3½" x 3½"

From the small-scale blue print, cut:
4 strips, 2½" x 42"
1 square, 4½" x 4½"
4 squares, 3½" x 3½"

From the red print for borders, cut:
2 strips, 1½" x 42"; crosscut into:
    2 strips, 1½" x 20½"
    2 strips, 1½" x 18½"
4 strips, 2½" x 42"; crosscut into:
    2 strips, 2½" x 32½"
    2 strips, 2½" x 28½"

Embroidering the Border Strips

1. Finger-press a beige tone-on-tone 5" x 21" strip in half widthwise to create a center fold. Open the strip and draw a small line in the bottom *seam allowance*, 1½" to the right of the fold. Measure 3" to the right of this line and draw another line as before. Draw a third line, 3" to the right of the last one. These lines indicate where to place the large daisy flower stems. Repeat on the left side of the strip, beginning 1½" to the left of the fold. Mark all four of the beige 21"-long strips in this manner.

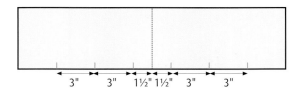

2. Using the pattern on page 79, trace the Garden Bed design onto the right side of the marked strips, lining up the daisy stem in the design with the small marked lines in the seam allowance. Trace each swirl flower only once, even if they don't overlap exactly; their alignment doesn't need to be perfect. Fuse the interfacing strips to the wrong side of the marked strips.

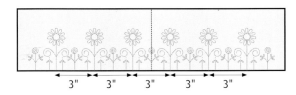

3. Using two strands of floss, embroider the designs following the stitch key and color guides on the pattern.

Assembling the Table-Mat Top

1. Centering the embroidery, trim the embroidered border strips to 4½" x 20½".

2. Lay out the 3½" squares in six rows of six squares each. Sew the squares together into rows. Press the seam allowances in opposite directions from row to row. Sew the rows together to complete the quilt center; press the seam allowances in one direction.

3. Sew the red 1½" x 18½" strips to the sides of the quilt. Press the seam allowances toward the strips. Sew the red 1½" x 20½" strips to the top and bottom of the quilt. Press the seam allowances toward the strips.

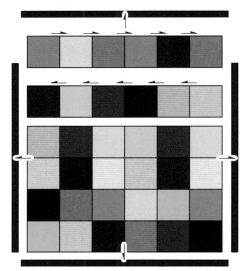

4. Sew two embroidered strips to the sides of the quilt, making sure the stems are toward the quilt edges. Press the seam allowances toward the red strips. Sew a green 4½" square to the left end of each remaining embroidered strip, and a blue 4½" square to the right end of each remaining embroidered strip. Press the seam allowances toward the squares to complete the pieced border strips. Making sure the stems are toward the quilt edges, stitch the pieced border strips to the top and bottom of the table mat. Press seam allowances toward the red strips.

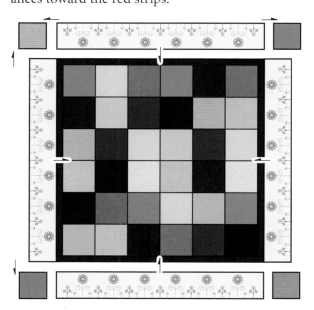

5. Sew the red 2½" x 28½" strips to the sides of the quilt. Press the seam allowances toward the strips. Sew the red 2½" x 32½" strips to the top and bottom of the quilt. Press the seam allowances toward the strips.

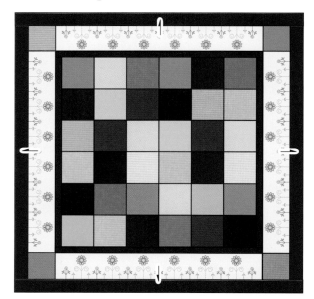

Quilt assembly

Finishing the Table Mat

1. Layer the quilt top, batting, and backing; baste. Using the pearl cotton and big-stitch quilting (see page 10), quilt an X in each center and border square. Quilt ¼" from the seam line in all red border strips. Trim the batting even with the quilt top.

2. Using the blue 42"-long strips, make and attach the binding *before* completing the quilting next to the binding seam.

Blanket stitch

Garden Bed Table Mat

Embroidery Key

⊂ Lazy daisy

● French knot

⊓⊓⊓ Blanket stitch

—— Backstitch

about the author

My name is Gail Pan, and I live on the outskirts of Melbourne, Australia, at the foot of the beautiful Dandenong Ranges (a series of low, verdant mountain ranges). Growing up in a home where sewing was always an important part of life, it was only natural that I tried every craft there was! I have always had some kind of project in the works, trying everything from knitting to cross-stitch. When my kids were little I made their clothes, and when they got too old for that, I moved on to patchwork. My design business was born out of my habit of always adapting whatever I'm working on until it becomes a new design altogether. In 2003, at the encouragement of some friends who were opening their own patchwork business, I began to design and release my own patterns. I have been designing ever since!

I teach all over the world and get great satisfaction and enjoyment from sharing my love of needle and thread. I have also met some amazing women whom I now can call friends. Happy stitching!